Learning Through The Seasons

Activities to Prepare Young Children for Success in School and a Lifetime of Learning

By Iris Katers, Esther Macalady,
Cheryl Anderegg, Jean Hetrick, and Tim Fox
Illustrated by Mark Nowicki
Cover Design by Josh Counter

Learning Through the Seasons

– An activity guide based on national standards to prepare young children for success in school and a lifetime of learning

– Written for grandparents, parents, teachers, and other caregivers using common materials in the home and community

© 2010 Grandparents Teach, Too

ISBN: 978-0-615-34442-3

Library of Congress Control Number: 2010903564

First Edition–2010

10   9   8   7   6   5   4   3   2

Published by Grandparents Teach, Too
Marquette, Michigan 49855

By Iris Katers, Esther Macalady, Cheryl Anderegg, Jean Hetrick, and Tim Fox
Illustrated by Mark Nowicki; Cover Design by Josh Counter
Printing collaboration by Avery Color Studios, Inc.

Dedication

Iris, Esther, Cheryl, Jean, and Tim wish to dedicate *Learning Through the Seasons* and all projects of Grandparents Teach, Too to our supportive families, students, and colleagues who have helped us on this journey.

We especially thank Dr. Tawni Ferrarini, Cohodas Chair and Director of the Northern Michigan University Center for Economic Education and Entrepreneurship; Nheena Weyer Ittner, Director of the Upper Peninsula Children's Museum; and Dr. Rodney Clarken, Associate Dean for Teacher Education and Director of School of Education, Northern Michigan University Marquette, Michigan.

We would also like to thank Jane Milkie Professor of Graphic Communication at Northern Michigan University, Marquette, Michigan; Jim Reeves and Bud Sargent of *The Mining Journal*; and Claudia Eliason and Loa Jenkins for their comprehensive and inspirational book for teachers of young children, *A Practical Guide to Early Childhood Curriculum (2008)*.

Introduction

Learning Through the Seasons is an activity guide for grandparents, parents, teachers, and other caregivers of young children. Each activity is based on national and international education standards for young children, but written for adults of every background. Each activity uses materials easily found in the home and community that make learning fun for young children and their loving adults.

How to Use this book

Read *Learning Through the Seasons* to learn what skills young children can develop by interacting with you during playtime every day. Find some ideas you would like to try with your child. Soon these activities will become a part of your daily routine. You will find new opportunities to combine fun and learning wherever you look.

You will notice that the activities in *Learning Through the Seasons* focus on the following:

Reading together daily.

Conversing throughout the day.

Developing skills to become readers, writers, and mathematicians.

Nurturing curiosity and skills in science, economics, geography, and history.

Getting along and helping others.

Learning to solve problems.

Enjoying art, music, and physical activity.

Inspiring creativity.

Being creative, curious, observant, and organized.

Making decisions.

Being self confident and respectful.

Learning where to find information.

Developing healthy eating and exercise habits.

Being a helpful and responsible family and community member.

Being eager to learn more.

Only you can create an environment in your home where young children will develop the skills and habits to ensure interest and success in school.

Helpful Tips for Raising Your Young Learners

Read together every day.

Have many opportunities for children to draw, cut, and color.

Restrict TV, video, and computer time.

Have give- and- take conversations often.

Listen to and sing all kinds of music.

Have books available for quiet times.

Provide opportunities for vigorous exercise.

Provide fruit and vegetable at meals and snacks time.

Encourage independence when appropriate.

Visit the library and various museums often.

Take every opportunity to instill self confidence.

Gently help—never push.

Playtime gives children opportunities to understand the world. It is an important vehicle for children's social, emotional, and cognitive development.

Children learn best in a community where they are safe, valued, their physical needs are met, and they are psychologically secure. — Abraham Maslow

Contents

Winter

Spring

Summer

Fall

Anytime Activities

Winter

1. How Do Children Understand New Ideas and Words?

Even everyday activities like getting dressed to go outside provide a good opportunity for learning. Understanding opposites, describing words, color and size words are important preschool language skills.

Materials:
outdoor clothing

What to Do:

This is a very simple activity you may repeat often during the colder months of the year. By talking through the process as you help dress your little ones to go outside, you will be teaching new words and important ideas. Use color words as you choose what hat or scarf to wear. Show your child a pair of mittens or boots is needed. Talk about the right one and the left one. Describe the clothes using words like fuzzy, smooth, wooly, striped, plaid, bumpy, soft, colorful, etc. Count the buttons, and show how zippers work—up and down, fast and slow. Use words like over, under, top, bottom, inside, outside, front, back, left, right, long, short. Make up a 'getting dressed' song by singing, "First we put on our snow pants. Next we put on our red sweater, then we put on our blue jacket." (The tune doesn't matter as long as you are having fun. A tune that works is "Here We Go Round the Mulberry Bush.")

What Other Activities Could We Do?

Sometimes, when you come back inside, use the same plan to describe things as you take off clothes and put them back where they belong. If your child is interested, take a few minutes to talk about what you did outside and maybe draw a picture and write a sentence together. Ask the librarian for some wintertime stories like *The Snowy Day or The Mitten*, and read them together.

2. Making a Simple Birdfeeder

Adults can help children develop a love of nature and a caring relationship with wildlife. Attracting birds to your backyard during the winter months can provide pleasure to people of all ages.

Materials:
wax paper
pinecones
soft peanut butter
birdseed
string or thin wire
knife or spreader

What To Do:

To help develop awareness, talk with your child about how birds need to find food in the winter months. Plan together to make a bird feeder, which can help attract birds to your yard. First, find some pinecones and lay them out on wax paper. Tie a string or wire about eight inches long around the cone, leaving string at the top to attach the birdfeeder to a tree later. Help to spread soft peanut better all around the cone. Next, sprinkle birdseed on the peanut butter. Refrigerating the cone will make it easier to handle. Hang it outside where you can watch the birds from an inside window. Later, check to see how many birds come to visit, or color pictures of different kinds of birds. Let your child tell others how to make this feeder. Help add works like first, next, last, etc. Find good books at the library about wildlife in winter.

How Will This Help My Child?

Children benefit from planning an activity and following the steps in the correct order to complete a project. By using words like first, second, next, finally or last, you will be helping to develop a sense of order or sequence. By talking together, answering questions and observing wildlife, you are stimulating natural curiosity. Spreading, rolling, patting, pouring, all help develop fine motor control.

3. Holiday Fun and Learning in the Kitchen

Holiday snacks are fun and easy to prepare even without a stove. Cooking together provides opportunities for varied hands-on activities and important conversations with adults that children need to become successful in school.

Materials:

sliced bread
jar of creamy peanut butter
bag of small pretzels
spreadable cream cheese
green food coloring
chocolate chips candy red hots (or dried
    fruit pieces)
table knife
doughnut cutter

What to do:

Spread plastic on your kitchen table and cover clothes to avoid a mess.

First, make a Rudolph Sandwich. Help children cut the crusts from five pieces of bread. Next, help them cut each piece of bread in half diagonally. You will have ten triangles of bread. Together carefully spread each triangle with peanut butter. Place them on a cookie sheet with the point facing the bottom and straight edge across the top. To make Rudolph's face, place a candy at the bottom tip of the triangle for a nose. Next, place two chocolate chips (or fruit) for eyes and two pretzels in each corner for antlers. The snacks are healthy, fun to make, and share.

Another easy snack is a cream cheese wreath. This snack is also made with sliced bread. Take turns using a doughnut cutter or cup and knife to cut a wreath shape out of the bread. Help children add a little green food coloring to the cream cheese and take turns stirring. After frosting the wreaths with cream cheese, place red hots or dried fruits around to look like berries.

Look for other simple recipes that allow children to do some of the work. Don't be concerned with appearance. They will think it's beautiful!

4. Fun in the Snow

Quality time can be spent outdoors just as well as indoors.

Materials:

winter clothing
good wet snow
large carrot
several BIG buttons
an old scarf and hat
two long sticks

What to do:

Experiment with the wet snow: notice if it sticks together, squeeze it in your fist. Explain that snow is made of water and when it is really wet we can build things with it.

Start with a small ball of snow in your hands and begin to roll it on the ground. Use words that describe size: big, bigger, biggest, small, smaller, smallest, large, larger, and largest. Roll that ball until it is perfect for the "bottom" of the snowman. Use words that describe position; bottom, middle, top, center and between. Make a second small ball and roll to make it "bigger". The "middle" part of the snowman is ready. Compare the snowballs. Lift it on top of the "largest" snowball. Roll the "smallest" ball for the "top".

Add a face; using some of the buttons add a smile at the "bottom" of the head, the carrot nose in the "middle" of the face, and 2 buttons for eyes. Wrap the scarf "between" the "smallest" and the "large" snowballs and place the hat on the "top" of head. Place two long sticks on each side of the "middle" snowball for arms.

How will this help my child?

Size and position words help build vocabulary and math skills. Rolling and lifting help develop gross motor skills.

What else can we do?

Make a snow family, placing them from smallest to biggest. Make each different: smiling, frowning, surprised, arms reaching skyward. Mix a drop of food coloring in a spray bottle and add clothing. **Be careful: food coloring stains clothing and skin.**

5. Indoor Active Games

Young children need daily exercise to develop large muscles in their arms and legs, especially during long stretches of chilly days. This sets the stage for a healthy lifestyle.

Materials:
beach ball
cardboard tubes
large storage container
paper plates
marker

What to do:

To avoid accidents, clear out any dangerous objects or play in a long hallway.

Throwing, Rolling, and Catching

Start on the floor rolling a beach ball back and forth with your legs shaped like a V to catch the rolling ball. Start close together and move farther apart keeping the experience successful. While seated, gently start throwing and catching instead of rolling.

To teach catching, use a large ball. Stand very close together and ease the ball into your child's arms. Gradually move farther apart. Children can also throw or roll a ball gently against a wall.

Other Indoor Sports:

To play basketball, throw a beach ball into a storage container.

Kickball is a good way to begin running bases. Make numbered bases out of paper plates taped to the floor. After kicking the beach ball, practice running around the bases together. Tap each one and say its number.

Soccer can also be played indoors with a beach ball and a large plastic storage container on its side.

Bowling is easy with a few plastic cartons and an old ball that has lost some of its air.

To play indoor hockey or golf, hit a beach ball with paper tubes reinforced with duct tape.

Call out colors on a Twister place mat and jump on them.

Play freeze tag. Call out a number, color, state, or letter (whatever you have been working on) to be able to move again. On a dark day, try flashlight tag. Instead of running, move in slow motion.

6. Having a Ball with Gravity

What goes up will come down with gravity. Adults caring for young children can easily combine play time conversation with teaching basic science concepts.

Materials:
beach ball or small squishy ball

What to do:

Tossing a beach ball up in the air or rolling it down a few stairs can be just plain fun. However, fun time can be turned into teaching moments when adults explain what goes up must come down. If a ball is thrown up, it will come down toward the larger object, the Earth.

Start out with your child a few steps up and the adult at the bottom. When you throw the ball, your child simply corrals it at the top and rolls it back down. As the ball rolls down, tell your child that gravity helps pull the ball down the steps.

Sometimes the ball will stop so you need to talk about pushing it harder. Other times there will be a little too much force and you'll need to talk about rolling more gently. This is a great time to count together, too, as the ball drops step by step.

Now switch places. Sit on the stairs at a point where your child can be successful getting the ball to you. Some children have a powerful throw from the start. Others will need more practice with the large muscles in their arms. No matter how far the roll, be sure to keep using that word "gravity" in conversation when the ball comes down.

What other activities could we do?

Gravity fun can also be taught by throwing leaves, snow, and water up in the air. While sliding at the park or sledding on a snowy hill remind children that gravity pulls them down.

7. Music and Movement

Just like exercise, young children need music every day. When adults turn on any kind of music or sing, young children naturally move and sing along.

Materials:

all kinds of music
cardboard and plastic containers
paper towel tubes
small ball
wooden spoons

What to do:

Music activities require neither specific skills nor special competence. Adults and children can enjoy peppy music in the morning and relaxing soft music at lunch, during car rides, before naps and bedtimes.

Marching Band and Exercise

John Phillip Sousa had it right! Sing a march and get moving. If you don't have marching music, go to www.youtube.com, and search for your favorite college band. Once you have the music, make some instruments. Drums are most popular and easiest to make. Find boxes, plastic containers, and wooden spoons.

The largest box can be a big bass drum. Smaller ones can be snare drums. Listen to the beat and drum together. Drum soft, loud, fast and slow. Try a kazoo (about $1). You can make a homemade kazoo by folding a piece of wax paper over the tooth edge of a comb and humming through the paper. For a trumpet, cover one end of a paper towel roll with wax paper and secure it with a rubber band. Punch a row of holes along one side of the roll with a pen tip. Hum into the open end while covering and uncovering hole to produce different sounds. To make chimes, tie washers on to a ruler and play with a spoon.

Pick up the drums and pretend to be called onto the football field. Marching is great exercise. March right, left, backwards, and turn around. Stop by a football game to watch the band or catch a band practice. Many cities and schools have band concerts.

8. More Music and Movement

Brain research suggests that music and movement help both sides of the brain work together.

Karaoke Fun

Children love to sing along. They learn words very quickly. Songs like "Bingo" drop off letters and keep everyone thinking. Don't limit them to typical children's songs. Children love show tunes, rock, country, jazz, patriotic, Latino, religious, holiday songs, or the latest children's movie tune. Most words are available free on line. Google® the song title, and you're ready to sing. Your public library has a variety of cd's and songbooks. If you don't know the words, do it Elmo's way—La, La, La, La.

Show Time

Create a show. Search closets for possible costumes and make a few instruments. For a maraca use two plastic cups filled with beans and duct taped together. Two aluminum pie plates with rope handles are excellent cymbals. An easy guitar is made with a small tissue box and four tough rubber bands around the box. Then duct tape the box to a ruler. Air guitars are just as fun. Make a microphone from a toilet paper tube, small ball, and of course, duct tape.

Once you've practiced, line up an audience of stuffed animals and announce in grand style. Invite guests over for pizza and short entertainment. Many children's museums have a stage, lights, and costumes just waiting for your next visit.

Dancing

Dancing is just as important. Children are all about movement. Turn on the radio and show them steps you know. Try some ballet steps. Move around the room. Children love to waltz or do a slow dance on your feet. Try a jitterbug and some fancy under the arm twirls. The polka, chicken dance, and Hokey-Pokey prepare young children for family gatherings. Clever adults use song and dance as part of bedtime preparation and toy pick up. The ABC (substitute counting numbers) song with a little dance works any time. Music is joy.

Spring

9. Science Walks

Adults love to take children for walks in springtime when plants begin to bloom and animals become more active. A walk is a great time to introduce concepts of "living" and "non-living."

Materials:

small drawing and writing notebook
paper
crayons or markers
magazines
scissors
glue

What to do:

Find a spot where you'll see both plants and animals. Explain that living things move, grow, and reproduce themselves. Together list and draw things children see that they think are alive. Explain that plants and animals are both alive, but they move and grow and reproduce in different ways. .

Pick up a rock and ask your children if it is living or not living. Make sure they understand that a rock cannot be alive because it cannot move or grow by itself or reproduce itself. Ask them to tell you something else that is not living like a swing set This might be harder than finding living things.

What else can you do?

Staple several pieces of paper to make a book. Together find five or six pictures of living or non-living things in magazines and cut them out in large circle shapes. Write a simple sentence on each page. (A robin is living. A mountain is not living.) After gluing each picture on the appropriate page, read the book together. Young children love "reading" along, knowing what each page says because of the picture.

How will this help my child?

Your children will begin to understand that some things are living and some things are not living expanding, their science vocabulary and knowledge. Cutting and gluing are good small motor activities. The best thing of all is the book you both have created. Your little ones will be able to read it and explain concepts they have learned.

10. Learning to Help Others

Grandparents and caregivers often need to do some work at home while the little ones are with them. Children love to help out with simple tasks.

Materials:
water
bucket
soap
sponge or cloth
hose
vacuum
broom, etc.

What To Do:

Job 1: Washing Up–Young children love to use water and soap bubbles to clean silverware, plastic dishes and cups. Set your little dishwasher up on a sturdy chair at the sink or use a big pan or wash pan on the table or floor. Show your children how to wipe off the table and chairs.

Job 2: Sorting Clothes–Let your children help you sort dirty clothes into piles of dark and light colors. Later, when the clothes are washed and dried, your children can help fold and sort again. (Matching socks is an especially good activity for learning about pairs as well as concepts of *same* and *different*.)

Job 3: Vacuuming and Sweeping–If you plug in the vacuum, or provide a broom or battery operated hand sweeper, your children will love to take turns pushing it around to gather up crumbs and dirt.

Job 4: Washing the Car–During the hot weather, this fun job is a big favorite. Set your children up with a hose, a bucket full of soapy water and a sponge or rag. Let them play in the water while they wet and clean and rinse the lower parts of the car. Be prepared for everyone to end up wet and happy.

Other jobs: Children can help with snow shoveling, knocking snow off of the doghouse, setting the table, dusting, providing food or water to pets, getting the newspaper or mail, watering plants, sweeping, or working in the garden.

How Will This Help My Child?

Be sure to give children work they can handle depending on their age and understanding, and be ready to finish up later if they get tired. Your young children will be developing language skills, muscle control, math and organizational skills, as well as a positive self-image that comes from helping others.

11. Weather Observation

Observing, investigating, and reporting the weather are good ways to nurture science thinking because weather affects play activities and clothing choices. By observing weather, many clothing arguments may be avoided.

What to do

Check out the weather every morning before breakfast to help plan for the day. Adults will be setting the stage for good breakfast conversation and building scientific vocabulary.

Check the temperature. Step outside or observe through a window. Will we need jackets, hats, and mittens today or can we dress for warm weather? Is it sunny or cloudy? Will we need to wear our sunglasses and hat?

Look at the sky. Is the sky really cloudy, partly cloudy, or clear? Are there clouds coming in? Observe the kinds of clouds. If the clouds are thick like a blanket and it's rather gray, stratus clouds are holding lots of possible moisture.

If it's a blue sky with some big white cotton ball cumulus clouds, it could be a nice day to play outside with proper clothing. If these puffy clouds are gray or black, we could have a storm.

If the sky is clear with just a few wispy cirrus clouds, we probably won't have moisture.

Observe the trees. Is it really windy, a little breezy, or a calm day? By observing weather many clothing arguments are avoided.

What else can I do?

Children love to paint weather pictures to hang on the refrigerator. You can also draw clouds, sun, or raindrops on a calendar to report weather. Compare your observations and predictions with professional forecasters.

If children have questions, like how clouds block the sun or what causes wind, go to www.ask.com or Google®.

Ask the librarian for help finding nonfiction (true) weather books with lots of colored pictures. Children also like Judi Barrett's *Cloudy with a Chance of Meatballs* and Tomie de Paola's *The Cloud Book*. Some children's museums have a TV weather studio to play weather reporter.

12. Rainy Day Project: Mixing Colors
Rainy days can be fun too!

Materials:
plastic cloth
coffee filters
red, yellow, and blue food coloring
small watercolor brush
clothespins (not the pinch kind)
container of water
OPTIONAL: pipe cleaners

What to do:
Cover the work area with the plastic cloth. Pick a color and paint on a coffee filter. Pick a second color and continue to paint on the coffee filter. Discuss what happens to the colors. Continue to experiment with the third color and discuss what happens. Take the opportunity to talk about "primary colors"(red, blue, yellow) and "secondary" (mixed colors). After painting on several coffee filters, let them air dry before proceeding.

Once the filters are dry, choose one and scrunch the middle together and place it inside a clothespin. Fan out the sides of the filter to make the wings of a butterfly. Cut the pipe cleaner in half and wrap that around the knob of the clothespin for antennae. Use the other filters to make more butterflies.

How will this help children?

Your child will discover that mixing two primary colors will make a secondary color and build vocabulary that artists use in creating designs.

Books to share:

Mouse Paint by Ellen Stohl Walsh, *The Very Hungry Caterpillar* by Eric Carle, *Charlie the Caterpillar* by Dom Deluise, and *Where Butterflies Grow* by Joanne Ryder.

13. Eye Catching Ground Level Birdbaths

Make your child's garden unique with ground level concrete birdbaths.

Materials:

rhubarb or hosta leaves
plastic wrap
spray cooking oil
vinyl patch concrete
paint
concrete sealer
gloves
brushes
containers
covered work table
paint shirt

What to do:

These fantastic birdbaths sit on the ground. They add surprise and color to your child's garden. Like any birdbath, change the water often to avoid hatching mosquitoes.

Gather large rhubarb or hosta leaves. Cover broken ones and holes with an overlap leaf and you won't know the difference. You'll need one bag of vinyl patch concrete for two large birdbaths.

Pile sand on the ground at least four inches thick and a few inches larger than the leaf. Smooth plastic wrap over the sand. Heavily spray the leaf with cooking oil. Place the leaf face down on the sand. Cut the leaf stem. Place another leaf face down on top pointing in the opposite direction. The more leaves you add, the deeper the birdbath will be. Mix up the concrete until it is like dough and pour it into the center of the leaf. Wear latex gloves to spread it out over the entire leaf. Generously cover the big veins that run down the middle. The concrete should be ¾ inch in the center and ¼ inch on the edges. Let it set for at least two days protected with a plastic tent. For extra sturdiness, leave it for about a week.

When dry, carefully lift and peel off the leaf. The edges will be fragile. Clean with a brush, prime it with two coats of primer. Paint with glossy deck paint, acrylic paint, or watercolors. Use concrete sealer to retain the color. Wear gloves, and paint outside. Store for the winter to avoid cracks.

What else can we do?

Draw a map of the garden. Place popsicle sticks with flower names to remember place-ment and learn the names. Put on a yucky face drawing for inedible plants.

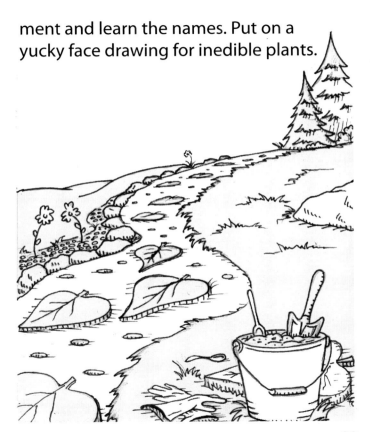

14. Gardening for Fun and Good Eating

Gardening is like magic to children. The activity increases science vocabulary, conversation skills, and teaches responsibility. Children have a better understanding of food production and learn about the wide variety of tasty fruits and vegetables available to eat. They also experience how adults find information and follow directions to be successful.

Materials:

child sized gloves
fast growing plants or seeds like mixed
   lettuce, peas, beans, sunflowers, cherry
   tomato, marigold, petunia, lamb's ear, or
   herbs

What to do:

Check out library books and magazines about plants and gardening. Draw pictures of plant parts, discuss their functions, and make a checklist of gardening jobs and needed materials. Draw a map and take pictures of the planting process.

Start a small project. Containers filled with plants listed provide a colorful patio garden if you don't have much space. Add a few annual plants for instant color.

If you have room, designate a section as your child's garden and together draw a garden plan. Leave enough room to weed and not step on plants.

Make a list. Shop for plants together and teach children how to select healthy looking ones. Read the labels and discuss what they mean. Read the back of seed packets and teach the correct names of plants and tools. Choose plants with the shortest growing season, appropriate plant hardiness zone, and amount of sunlight for your space.

When you are ready to plant, check off your list, read, and follow directions. This shows your child that reading and writing are important and useful.

While waiting for the plants to grow, your child can help weed and water the rest of the garden. Once the flowers bloom, teach your child to pinch off the dead flowers (dead-heading) to encourage more buds to form.

If little trees sprout in your yard, transplant one to a better spot, and let it grow.

Place small squares of bath soap several feet apart to keep critters away.

Summer

15. Water Play

Water is a great source of easy fun and learning activities.

What to do:

Head to the beach with different sized storage containers, buckets, shovels, and plastic toys. Take along a plastic bag to clean up the area, too. Gather flat rocks on the beach and teach your children to skip them in the water.

Place some water in a container and start adding a few stones. Guess and count how many stones it takes before a container overflows. Gather natural items found on the beach and find out what floats and sinks. Children also like to fill a small plastic boat- like container with rocks and estimate how many are needed to sink it.

Indoor water fun:

Water play is easy indoors, too. Fill a dishpan or sink with water. Use plastic measuring cups to fill different containers. Keep the water warm and the flow very low. Place towels on the sink edge and on the floor under the chair to sop up some of the mess. Dolls, trucks and other toys can be washed with a little dish soap and a brush if you don't plan to use the water for plants later.

Bath time

Bath time can an educational and practical activity. Children learn about objects that float and sink. Estimate how many objects will fit in different containers before they sink.

Paint with Water

Water is a cheap paint, too. Young children love to paint with water and a small brush on paper. Provide a bucket and different kinds of large paintbrushes. Together make the ABC's, numbers, shapes, and draw pictures on the driveway. Remember to explain that the water molecules evaporate into the air.

Cleaning Windows

Children love to clean windows. Thoroughly rinse out spray bottles and refill with water. Teach children how to spray the windows and wipe with squeegees and hand towels.

16. Keeping Your Child Happy and Learning in the Car

Car seat time can be frustrating for everyone if you don't plan for the trip. Verbal car games help children recall facts, compare, categorize, read signs, count items, listen and take turns.

What To Do:

One game is called "What Do You Know?" The adult makes up simple questions and children take turns giving their answers. Questions are based on the age/interest/vocabulary and experience level of each player. For example, an adult asks younger children," How many colors do you know?" "What are the names of the people in our family?" "What are the names of the seasons?" "What foods are orange?" "What do we call a person who takes care of us when we get sick?" "Who grows food for our grocery stores?"

For the older child, the questions could be related to geography, history, etc. "How many states can you name that begin with the word new?" or "How many bird names can you remember?" "Name a holiday for each season." "What is 9 X9?" Once you get started, you will think of many possible questions.

Another car game is called, "I'm Thinking of Something" (pick a color). Children watch out the window to find something this color.

Reading signs is a great way to encourage signal and word awareness. "Can you find a sign with a number or an arrow or the name of a store?" "Can you find a sign that starts with the letter "S", etc.?"

What else can I do?

Sing favorite songs or look for cows, horses, and trucks of a certain color. Retell a favorite storybook or movie. Discuss favorite foods or places to visit. Think about how two things are the same or different. Example:" How are a bird and an airplane the same (or different)?"

17. Enjoying picture books

Experts agree that reading to your young child is extremely important. Most children who are read to on a daily basis will be ready to learn to read on their own, and they will develop a rich vocabulary as well as a love of books.

Materials:

any books with pictures
cloth or plastic board books for the
   youngest children
magazines, colorful books from home or
   the library

What To Do:

Every day, during the day, at nap and bedtime, sit close with your children. When possible, let them choose the books. Often children like to hear the same book over and over again. Talk about the cover. What is the title? Who is the author? Show how to hold the book and turn the pages as you go. Look at the pictures, guess what is going to happen, talk about the characters. Sometimes point to the words as you read along. Encourage questions, and let your children join in to say the fun parts or name things. What is your favorite part? Which pictures do you like best? How do pictures and words get into a book? Older kids will enjoy hearing you read from kid's magazines or longer picture/story books.

Teach your children how to take care of books. Have the books available for children to use again on their own. A special box or low shelf for the books is a good idea.

How Will This Help My Child?

Children need to hear the sounds and patterns of our language. They need to know letters and words carry meaning, and stories have a beginning, middle and end. All this crucial learning can be obtained in a very natural pleasurable way when you enjoy picture books and stories together.

18. Picnic Fun and Learning

Summer is the perfect time for a picnic. Your young child will love the excitement of planning for and participating in this traditional outdoor experience.

Materials:

picnic materials:
blanket
plates
bags
drinks
bread, peanut butter, jelly or other
    sandwich food
carrots, fruits, eggs, cookies
plastic knife
peeler
camera

What To Do:

Plan a picnic lunch together. With your child watching, print a list of the things you would like to bring. What are some good picnic foods?

Do you need to buy some things at the store?

If you are making sandwiches, your children can help spread on the butter, mayonnaise or peanut butter and jelly. Talk about cutting the sandwiches in halves, fourths or different shapes.

With a little help, children can peel the carrots, wash the fruit, and place things in plastic bags or containers. You can make cookies together or buy some before picnic day. Read and follow directions on the frozen drink can. Pack up the bag or basket. Check the list together by reading it out loud.

Once outside, pick a good place in the yard to spread out the blanket and set up the food. Let your children give everyone serving utensils. While you are eating, look around. What kind of summertime plants do you see? How is the weather?

After lunch, if there is sand close by, make a square, rectangle, circle, semi circle, rhombus, triangle, and diamond in the sand.

How Will This Help My Child?

Planning and setting up a sequence of activities is an important learning skill. In addition, children are developing fine motor skills while peeling vegetables and making sandwiches. They are learning about the seasons, too.

19. Teaching Economics Problem Solving

Finding ways to creatively solve problems and find alternatives are important skills. Role-playing a young ice cream entrepreneur with business problems provides fun and economics learning.

Materials:
pretend ice cream counter
United States map
play money

What to do:

Set up a pretend ice cream or lemonade counter in the backyard. Take turns being storeowners and customers as you act out an economics play.

Children store owners and adult customers ask for their favorite ice cream. The storeowners make up problems. This time, they are out of the flavor. The children come up with a few suggestions to solve the problem. Some problems and solutions are realistic. Some are preschool silliness. Call the ice cream factory and send over ice cream with a NASCAR driver. Unfortunately, the whole city is out according to the person on the phone! What can they do?

Adults and children go on a pretend computer to contact someone in a different state. It will take three days. They check out the map and the route for the truck. The sale is lost today because the customers go to another ice cream store. The truck arrives and the customers return to the store the next day because the owners have such good and friendly manners.

More problems come up. The cost of ice cream goes up if there isn't much left. The power goes out in a storm and the ice cream melts. The health department shuts them down because of ants. There is competition from another store. The truck gets lost and calls for directions. The children get very excited thinking of solutions.

What else can I do?

Setting up scenarios on car trips keep everyone involved while the family thinks of humorous problems and solutions. Imaginary zoos, grocery stores, and hikes are great role-plays to solve problems and build vocabulary.

20. Learning about Summer Butterflies and Moths

Mid summer brings butterflies to our gardens. Their appearance provides an introduction to the wonders of insect life. Young children can learn the important parts of an insect, information about life cycle changes, and have fun while they develop better eye-hand coordination with these easy art projects.

Materials:
tissue and construction paper
yarn or string
pipe cleaners (optional)
rubber band
stick
scissors
paints
easy books about butterflies

What To Do:
Watch for butterflies and moths in your yard. Notice the colors, shapes, and symmetry of the body.

Inside, read some information books about insects or the fiction book *The Very Hungry Caterpillar* by Eric Carle. Construct a make-believe butterfly. Take several pieces of tissue paper, fold them in half, and cut the edges off to make a rounded shape like the wings of a butterfly. Use the string or yarn to pull the pieces together in the middle to make the body. Pipe cleaners can be glued on to make antennae. Point out the different parts of the insect as you put it together. Play catch with the butterfly, or attach it to a small stick to fly it around.

A project for another day could be to make another kind of colorful butterfly. To teach symmetry, fold a piece of paper in half and cut a big butterfly wing shape through the double paper. (Younger children will need help to do this part.) Place a few dots of paint of different colors inside the folded shape and press the two wings together. Open, and tape the butterfly to the window or refrigerator.

21. Fireworks on Paper

The Fourth of July is a great family time to build traditions and memories. The activities are often hectic and loud. For a break, create fireworks art and discuss the holiday.

Materials:
white paper
water color paints
brushes
water
flat plastic plates for water
straws

What to do:

Pass out supplies. Dip a paintbrush in water and one primary color of red, yellow, or blue.

Place a LARGE watery drop of one primary color on the paper. The drop must be raised and not allowed to soak into the paper. Then quickly place a drop of another primary color a quarter inch away.

Blow the one color toward the other with the straw. One giant burst of air creates a splat. Blowing from the side with the head near the table creates a different effect. Keep blowing the paint as it divides into branches of color that mix together until they won't spread any more. Cover the whole page with explosions of color.

Discuss how the colors mix. Red and blue make purple, red and yellow make orange, blue and yellow make green.

Think of the sounds fireworks make like pow, bang, crack, sizzle, ka-boom, and ka-pow. Print the sounds (onomatopoeia) on the paper.

Start a conversation about the holiday. What do we do on the Fourth of July? Why do you think we use fireworks and have parades? Is this a happy or sad time? Why is the Fourth like a big birthday party for the United States? Discuss why Americans celebrate. Depending upon your children's ages, you can use your knowledge of 1776 and the desire to be free from England.

Children can dictate a family story to you and use the art for a cover.

Visit the library together and check out books about colors, parades, celebrations, famous people, and history.

22. Where in the World Do I Live?

Map exploration can be used to show where a child lives and teach geography.

Materials:

map of your area (often found in a
   phone book)
state map
U.S. map
world map
globe

What to do:

Using the local map, find your child's street. Point out familiar sites like the library, grocery store, a park, or a museum. Talk about your street and the city where your child lives. Help your child learn the home address by repeating the street name and the city often.

On another day use the state map and show where your city is on the map. Use the state map to point out some familiar sites like a local lake. Practice saying the address and now add the state.

Use another day to show the U. S. map and point out your state. Point out a few interesting places, such as Disneyworld, where the President lives, or a state with lots of sunshine. Talk about the oceans that border the shores of our country. Again practice the address and this time add our country.

Using the map of the world, find our country and backtrack to find the state and city (if possible). Use the globe to discuss that the earth is not flat. Point out where Santa lives and the route he takes to get to your house. Point out the other side of the world where penguins live.

Daevin Scillian's *P is for Passport: A World Alphabet* is a great one.

How will this help young children?
Young children get a glimpse into the big picture of the world. It introduces maps and how to use them.

What else can I do?
Google® maps and show your child the world, state, city and street from space. Zoom in and find your house. Libraries have many books about maps, your area, state and country.

23. POP! Bubbles are for Fun and Learning

A warm sunny day is a good time to "play" with bubbles.

Materials:

gather some objects with holes
flat shallow container to hold the bubble
  mixture
bubble mixture:

To make the mixture gently stir ¼ cup liquid dishwashing detergent, ¾ cup cold water, and 5 drops of glycerin. The glycerin makes the bubbles stronger and can be purchased at most drugstores. The solution gets better with age so you may want to mix it the day before.

What to do:

Use some objects like a fly swatter, a colander, slotted spoon, apple slicer, straw, and a spatula with holes to place in the bubble mixture. You could also use pipe cleaners and a hanger that has been bent to form circles. Pour some of the bubble mixture into the shallow, flat container and cover the remaining mixture to use on another day. Dip and wave each object, discuss the size of the bubbles, how many bubbles are formed from each object, and why some objects work better than others. Twirl to see if that makes the bubbles different. Try to catch bubbles on an object or your hands. Study a caught bubble till it breaks. What colors do you see? How big is the bubble?

How will this help children?

Experimenting is a great way to explore your child's world. It allows for rich discussion on predicting and the outcome. Experimenting also involves problem solving.

What else can I do?

You can add food coloring to the bubble mixture and discuss what happens. Visit the local library to look for books about bubbles. A few suggestions are *Bubble Trouble* by Mahy and Dunbar, *Bubble Trouble* by Huime and Cressy, *Benny's Big Bubble* by O'Connor and dePaola, and *Bubble Bath Pirates* by Krosoczka.

24. Science Fun and Learning with Spider Webs

Opportunities for learning happen right outside your window. Observing spiders and other animals help children form science questions, search for answers at the library, increase vocabulary, learn to converse with adults, sketch, and make their own books.

Materials:

magnifying glass	drinking straw
spider library books	string
paper	sand
glue	bread
tape	peanut butter
black marker	pretzels
scissors	
black paper,	

What to do:

What can you do with a spider? Take out a magnifying glass for several days and watch while it constructs its web, collects insects, and possibly encases them. Watch the spider at night with flashlights. Investigate your yard to compare webs.

Check out some spider books from the library like *I Love Spiders* by John Parker and *Anansi the Spider* by Gerald McDermott. Look for books with many colorful pictures. Then read the picture captions and summarize information. Be sure to discuss appearance, web, and food. What are its enemies, habitat, and interesting behaviors? Try to discover what kinds of spiders you have been observing.

Your children can keep a science journal with sketches and their words dictated to you and carefully printed. Read their words back to them and point under the words in a smooth flowing manner.

Encourage children to use geometric shapes like circles and parts of lines called line segments when they sketch or draw webs on paper or in sand.

Since art develops fine motor skills, create your own spiders. Cut out two black circles for the head and body, eight long skinny rectangles, and glue them together. Tape the spider on half a straw. Place a long string through the straw so the spider can climb and drop down. Attach both ends of the string to objects so the spider can move and climb.

Together you can make edible spiders by cutting two circles from bread, spreading peanut butter, and adding eight pretzel legs and raisins eyes.

25. Fun and Exercise

Superheroes, fairy tales, and cartoon characters are inspirations for imaginative play and large motor exercise. Think up a story and go outside for an hour of daily exercise. Healthy children use the large muscles of the arms, legs, and trunk to jump, hop, skip, kick, throw, catch, dance around, balance, push, pull, or jog.

What You Need:
park equipment
nature path
yard, or beach

What to do:

Young children enjoy exercise more when it's fun and imaginative. They imagine being stiff legged robots, galloping horses, soaring birds or characters with magical super human powers. To prepare, do some stretching first.

Then act out a story your young children know. Perhaps there is an animal to rescue, but there are all kinds of obstacles in your way. There may be an invisible line, overturned log, or 2X4 to walk on. Play "Follow the Leader" to avoid getting stuck in the muck or some other danger. Throw a magic stone or stick at a tree to break through an invisible barrier. Jump over a large stone or climb on a tree stump to look around. Gather sticks to make a safe path to hop on, or write a secret message with shapes and letters in the sand. Jog from one object to next.

Skip stones in the water. Pick up large rocks to make towers or walk along the beach and hunt for rocks, sticks, and other beach treasures.

Make an obstacle course around the yard. Set up a board as a balance beam. Roll a beach ball around, play soccer, catch, shovel, or sweep the sidewalk. Lay a rope on the ground for children to jump over or walk between.

Children love to play "What time is it, Mr. Fox," "Red Light/Green Light," and many kinds of freeze or flashlight tag games. When someone is tagged, the person says a story character, color, letter, names a state, spells a word, or counts.

26. Sandbox Geography and History

While children play in the sandbox teach them a little geography, history, and imaginative storytelling, too.

Materials:

sand shovels
pails
plastic people
dinosaur or other animal sets
cars and trucks
Legos®
sticks for trees
vinegar
baking soda
dish detergent
red food coloring
pie pan
tin foil

What do I do?

Decide the kind of geographic features you will create with your child. Will it be your community, western mountains, Great Lakes, river basin, plains with roads, a cityscape with buildings and rivers, an island with a volcano, or an imaginary planet? Will the period of history be time of the dinosaurs, castles, in the future? Where will your imagination take you? Many children like to rescue or act out a story they have heard.

Geographic features might include mountain ranges, roads through mountain passes, coral reefs, plateaus, an isthmus, islands, archipelagos, peninsulas, plains, basins, or steppes. If you don't mind a sandy mess and your sand box dries out well, add a few water features like wetlands, straits, oceans, gulfs, glaciers, deltas, lakes, bays, harbors, canals, channels, and a river's source and mouth. Just choose a few that fit your plan. Otherwise, save the water features for the beach.

Build, converse, and make decisions together. Use the geographical terms and start your imaginary story about plastic figures, cars, and trucks

If you want a volcano in the sandbox, make a six-inch high tin foil cone with a bottom so it doesn't leak. Place it in a pie pan. Mix ½ cup vinegar, red food coloring, and dish detergent. Pour the mixture in the tin cone. Add a tablespoon or more of baking soda to the cone for eruption. The first time you do this, your child may only want to make volcanoes for the rest of playtime.

Fall

27. A Wonderful Day with Apples

Apples can help teach children to observe, use their senses, make choices, and predict. All are skills used in science and language activities. They can teach how to weigh materials and create fractions. Discussing food costs is a beginning economic principle.

Materials:

apples
table knives
red, green, and yellow poster paint

What to do:

At the grocery help children pick out four apples of different colors. Weigh the apples on the produce scale. Check the numbers to see which one weighs most. At the checkout look at the prices to see which apple is most expensive. Talk about why some apples might cost more. At home look at a map to see where apples are grown.

Before working with the apples, teach children to wash apples and their hands. Carefully cut the different colored apples in half from the stem through the core. Discuss halves as two equal pieces. Children can predict the apple with the best taste and then sample pieces of each color. After they decide which apple they like best, discuss words like sweet, sour, and crunchy. Match the words to the different apples.

Cut the extra apple so the stem is at the top of the first half. Children are always excited to see the seeds in the center in the shape of a star.

Get out some red, yellow and green poster paint. Dip the halves in paint and have the children make apple prints. They love to see the little star on the prints.

Apples make a nutritious snack. Cut them very thin and add a little cinnamon for something different.

Make applesauce or apple cookies. Some wonderful books about apples include *The Apple Pie Tree* by Zoe Hall and *Johnny Appleseed* by Steven Kellogg.

28. Fun with Homemade Masks

Young children love to dress up and pretend. Throughout the year play with old masks, make new ones or design a character headband. This is a "do together" project as some of the planning, cutting and gluing may require your help.

Materials:

medium brown paper bag
construction paper
glue
stapler
crayons or markers
scissors
small decorations like feathers, buttons,
    ribbon, yarn, string—also fun things to
    wear like hats, ear muffs, and aprons

What To Do:

Paper masks: After talking with your child about what he would like to pretend to be, help him color and decorate a white paper plate or medium paper bag. Cut out holes for eyes and nose. Yarn can be glued on for hair. Pieces of colored paper can be stapled on to make noses, whiskers, or ears. Young children often prefer to hold a mask in front of their face with a tongue depressor or stick, rather than have it tied on to their head.

Ski hat masks: Using an old soft ski hat, you can cut out holes for eyes and nose, decorate, and pull it down over the head.

Headbands: Headbands rather than facemasks often work best for young children. Make a face or hat with colored paper, decorate with other paper pieces or add feathers. Then measure a strip of paper to fit your child's head. Staple the strip to the decorated part for a face-free "mask".

Using props: Sometimes the best pretend clothing might be just an apron, shawl, glasses or special hat. Children can pretend to be TV, cartoon or story characters, construction workers with hard hats, animals, cowboys, princesses, pilgrims, chefs, farmers, carpenters, doctors, astronauts, or firemen with just a little help from you. This is a great time to take a photo to show to others or write a story.)

How Does This Help My Child?
When children pretend, they are developing imagination, using background knowledge and building vocabulary.

Drawing, cutting, gluing, and coloring all help to build small muscle control.

29. Science and Exercise

Young children love to have an outing in the yard or neighborhood. Taking walks gives children a chance to appreciate the outdoors while improving fitness, building language, and learning at the same time.

Materials:
bag
several paper plates
glue

What to do:

Take a walk outside. Together, collect a variety of colorful leaves and put them in a bag. As children collect leaves, talk about the different colors and shapes. Some are rounded. Some have points.

At home sort out two or more paper plates. Show how you glue a red leaf on one plate and a brown leaf on another plate. Older children can work with three to five colors, so you may add orange, dark brown, and yellow, depending on the type of trees you see.

Then, pick a leaf out of the bag and decide together which plate has a matching leaf—red or brown. Gently help as necessary to place and glue all matching leaves on the correct plate. All other leaves can go into a "no match" bag.

Talk about the colors of all these leaves on each plate. If children are working mostly alone to sort the leaves, check over the plates before gluing. Stop when children lose interest or become tired.

How will this help my child?

Matching and sorting are important pre-math skills. Color recognition and naming the colors are expected in kindergarten. Gluing, like all other art related activities, builds small muscle skills in the fingers, as well as, eye-hand coordination.

What else can I do?

Play a matching game with clothes. For example, "Which color plate has leaves the same colors as your shirt?" Count the color plates you have completed while touching each one. At the library, ask for books about leaves, fall or colors.

30. Graphing Halloween Candy

Here's a " good" use for all that Halloween candy.

Materials:

child's collected Halloween candy
large piece of paper or poster board, which
 has a previously drawn graph on it
 (several vertical columns of two inch
 squares, equal distance from each other
 all the way up the columns)

What to do:

After dumping the candy on a flat surface, separate into piles of candy by type. Carefully, print the type of candy for each column in the bottom box based on the piles of separated candy. Column one can be the child's favorite type of candy. Place the second favorite candy in column two, etc. Discuss the various sizes, shapes and colors. When all the candy has been placed on the graph, it is time to discover and discuss what the bar graph shows. First, count each type separately. What type has the most? What type has the least? Are there two that are the same height? Why do you think people give out more of one type of candy? Point how easy it is to talk about something when materials are organized in a graph rather than in a big pile.

How will this help my child?

Graphing helps with counting, organizing,

and comparing objects of different attributes. It also increases math and science vocabulary and thinking skills.

What else can I do?

Graph by sizes, with or without nuts, gum flavors or colors. Graph other objects like small cars, Legos®, cereal, money, rocks on the beach, or leaves. A few books about graphing are *More or Less, Three Little Firefighters, Dave's Down-to-Earth Rock Shop* by Stuart J. Murphey and Tana Hobin's *More, Fewer, Less.*

31. Pumpkin Poetry

Children can write their first poetry using the five senses, with a little help from you. They'll have pumpkin poetry cards to send to relatives around Halloween and many new vocabulary words.

Materials:

pumpkins or jack o' lanterns
gourds
baked pumpkin product
construction paper
newsprint, markers
crayons
children's scissors

What to do:

Cover the entire space with paper for writing and drawing. Whole pumpkins work well for sight and sound. Pumpkin pieces are great for smell and touch. Pumpkin baked goods are mighty fine for tasting.

Help children write words or draw images that represent their feelings using their senses. As they draw, and talk about their feelings, print their words carefully using correct form on the paper. Remind them to look, smell, and touch inside and out. Encourage them to thump the pumpkin.

What might this pumpkin say if it could talk about the five senses? "I smell like earth. I taste like a thousand orange rainbows. I feel squeezy, squishy, and squirmy. I look like a giant golden nugget. I have smiling lines all around me."

These words from young children have a poetic ring. Without exception, young children are amazed to discover the poet that has been hiding inside them as they express the qualities of ordinary objects.

Now read the words and arrange them to sound more fun, poetic, and musical.

Here is an example written by an adult and young child.

Pumpkin

Giant golden nugget,
Smells like earth,
Squishy, squeezy, squirmy,
Smiles surround it.

Tastes like a thousand orange rainbows

How does this help my child?

Young children discover the wonder of words through writing poetry about ordinary objects like eggs, broccoli, socks, rocks, bagels, toast, favorite toys, blanket, leaves, and snow.

32. Thanksgiving Celebrations

Sometimes young children are a little "lost" in all the preparations and hubbub of Thanksgiving. With a little planning, families can set up a simple way to include children and keep them busy during meal preparation. Children will be learning about seasons, holidays, and how everyone needs to help in a family. They will be developing thoughtfulness and an appreciation for nature.

Materials:
colored leaves pressed in a book
gourds or small pumpkins
pinecones
dried corncobs
fall flower blossoms
vine with berries

What To Do:

Designate a few older children and adults to talk with your young ones about a very special job they can do to help with this fall tradition. Suggest that all family members will have a chance to say something they thankful for, and everyone will place a decoration from nature on the center of the table to make it look pretty. Give children a chance to think, discuss, and practice what they plan to say ahead of time. Don't forget to thank all the helpers!

Gather materials and place all the things on a tray. On the day of the dinner, let children pass out a few items to each person at the table.

Once the family is seated, take a minute or two for all people at the table to mention something they are thankful for and to place their decorations in the tray or basket.

What else can I do?

Talk about the seasons, especially the fall and how the things that have been growing all summer are ready to eat. How is nature getting ready for winter? Children can also count the number of people and set the table with napkins and silverware. Are there one place and one chair for each person? Count them.

33. Family Tree with Little Hands

A perfect family Thanksgiving activity is to create a family tree. It's a great project for every family member.

Materials:

a large sheet of construction paper
smaller pieces of colored paper
child size scissors
glue
markers
crayona
 family and pet photos

What to do:

Draw the tree with a trunk and branches using the markers and crayons. Get ideas from everyone. Even young children will have fun coloring the bark. Children and adults can trace and cut out their hands. Some of the younger children will need help. After the hands are cut out, everyone should write his or her own name on the hand before it is glued to the tree. Older children can write the names of toddlers and babies. They'll like to help with that. The hands will be the leafy part of the tree. You can put individual pictures on each hand or place them under the tree. Be creative and accept ideas from everyone. You can even make paw prints for pets and put pictures of them on the tree, too. Write special things about family members on their hands. This will be a work of art with each child and adult adding something unique.

You could even frame the project and hang it on the wall in your home.

How this will help my child?

Working together helps young children learn to share and help each other. Thinking of special things about family members and writing them can develop literacy skills. Tracing, cutting, and gluing are important fine motor skills for young children.

What else can I do?

Anything done as a family creates a bond between family members. Children love doing projects with other family members and going on family outings.

Anytime Fun and Learning

34. Science and Planting Bulbs

Preparing for winter by planting a few flower bulbs is another opportunity to teach young children science, geography, economics vocabulary, converse with adults, and beautify the neighborhood.

Materials:
children's gloves
small shovels or large spoons
garden bulbs
bone meal
rolled up towel to kneel on
paper and crayons for a map
leaves for mulch
water

What to do:

Check out a few children's books about flowers and bulbs so you learn the science of bulbs. Explain that together you are planting bulbs to surprise everyone in spring.

Walk around the yard and discuss where some bulbs could be planted based on good soil, water, sunshine, and visibility through windows. Sketch a map.

Shop together for bulb varieties like tulips, daffodils, hyacinths, narcissus, crocus, and alliums. Discuss colors and check that the bulbs look healthy and fresh. (This is an example of good economics teaching because you are making a PLANNED purchase from a list.) Also, discuss that animals like to eat bulbs and flowers. If you have many animals, you might want to stick to daffodils and narcissus. Animals may also move your bulbs around.

Using proper upper and lower case letters, carefully print a list of gardening materials. Gather them while your child checks off the list.

Read the planting directions on the back of the package out loud and follow them exactly. Who will do each step? What is a bulb, and how does it work? What will grow from the pointed side of the bulb (stem)? What will grow from the round bottom side (roots)? Then create a planting assembly line. Cover up the hole with soil and leaves. Give it a few gentle "love pats". Water well.

What else can I do?
Volunteer together for a community beautification project.

35. Homemade Play Dough and Changing Activities Without a Fuss

Prepare young children for preschool and still get some work done around the house.

Materials:
kitchen timer
play dough
kitchen drawer items

What to do:

1. Choose a timer.

2. Choose an activity like making play dough. Set the timer for one hour and give your children 100% of your attention. Explain what you are going to do and play together until the timer rings.

3. Make the recipe to the right. With help, children can measure the ingredients, stir, and choose food coloring. Let the dough cool and knead it well.

4. While the dough cools in the refrigerator, collect a container of play dough toys: cookie cutters, measuring cups, spoons, plastic silverware, a cookie sheet to work on, muffin tin, and plates for serving pretend food. Find trucks to cart away play dough food and other materials to the grocery store in a play dough city you construct. Leave time to play.

5. Five minutes before the timer rings, remind children the timer will ring shortly and that means your playtime together is finished. When the timer rings, remind them they may continue playing while you do some work around the house.

6. Set the timer for the amount of time you need. Children may want to play with puzzles or art supplies instead of play dough. When the timer rings, it's time to change the activity. They have been playing quietly so it's time to run around and be active. (See large motor activities.)

How will this help my children?

Setting time limits with a timer helps them go from one activity to the next. They learn a sequence of activity, stop, and change to a new activity without a fuss. Playing with play dough builds fine motor skills and imagination.

NEVER FAIL PLAY DOUGH RECIPE

1 cup flour
½ cup salt
1 tablespoon cream of tartar
1 tablespoon cooking oil
1 cup water
food coloring

Mix all ingredients together in a 3 qt. saucepan. Cook and stir over medium heat until mixture begins to stick together. Remove from heat. Cool slightly. Begin kneading. Store in plastic bags.

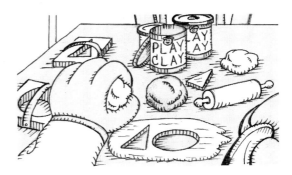

36. How Do Children Become Writers?

When children begin to understand that they can put their words and ideas down on paper, they are on their way to becoming writers. At first, young children use drawing and scribble writing. As they develop more muscle control and a little awareness of the importance of letters, they may print strings of letters across the page. Soon they will learn that sounds and letters can be printed to make words.

You have a wonderful opportunity to model writing, develop your children's vocabulary, and foster interest in self-expression.

Materials:
sheets of white paper
crayons
pencils

What To Do: Make a picture poster

Be sure your young children have many opportunities to scribble and draw with pencils, crayons, and washable markers. Sometimes children will want an older child or adult to draw with them. First, talk together about what to draw. Maybe they will want to draw other members of the family, their pets, or friends. Help plan the picture and encourage drawing and coloring. Make up a simple sentence together. PRINT your child's words carefully at the top or bottom of the paper using lower case (not caps) letters except when appropriate. Sometimes, you may just label things in the picture by printing the word next to an item. When you are finished, point to the words and read them out loud several times. Be sure to print your child's name on the paper. Put the picture on the refrigerator or encourage "reading" it to others.

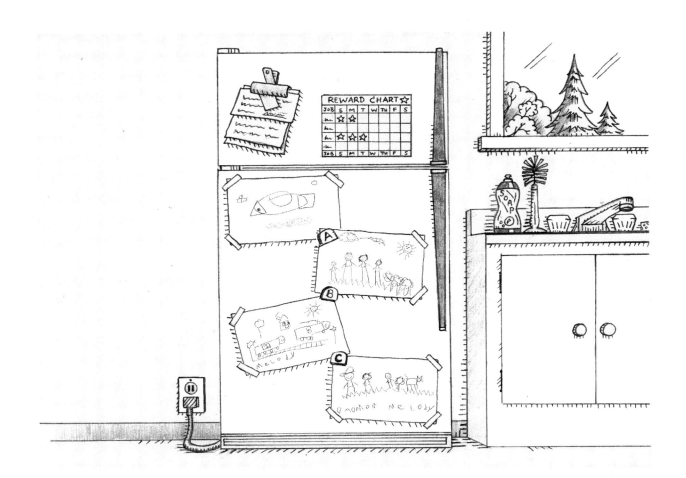

37. Becoming a Writer: Pictures, Posters, and Collages

Talking, remembering, reading, and writing together are important activities to develop language. Children become writers as they realize they can use marks on a paper to stand for ideas. With you as their first model and teacher, children who experiment and practice communicating through writing at home will be successful writers in school.

Materials:

pencils
paper
glue
photos of family, pets, or trips

What To Do:

To make a picture poster, find some photos of your family, pets, or a family trip. Spend some time talking about the photos and choose a few favorites. Help your child glue one or two pictures on a sheet of paper. (Leave lots of space between the photos.) Make up a simple sentence about the picture. Using your child's words and ideas, PRINT a sentence under each photo. (Use capital letters only for beginning the sentence or names.) When you are finished, point to each word as you read the sentences out loud. Hang the paper up on the refrigerator or wall for everyone to see.

What Other Activities Could I Do?

If you have more time, you can make a little book using a photo on each page and a printed simple sentence that your child has asked you to write. Make the printing big and clear on each page. Staple or clip several pages together. You might want to make a cover for the booklet with a simple title and your child's name on the front. Read the book together and add it to your storybooks. It could also make a wonderful gift.

38. Becoming a Writer

It is magical when children understand they can put their ideas down on paper, and we can save our ideas for reading later on. Children benefit from seeing adults writing.

Materials:

paper
pencils
crayons

What To Do:

Make a list. It could be a "to do list" for daily chores, packing for a trip, a birthday party, or grocery list. Sit together and explain that you are going to write a list. Decide out loud what you need to do or buy. PRINT each item on your paper. Children may just want to watch, or perhaps they may want to make their own lists at the same time. Encourage holding a pencil or crayon correctly and pretend-writing. Don't worry about making letters perfectly or spelling. However, if your children are older and interested in letters, help with beginning sounds and letter formation. Talk about and read the ideas you have written. Save your lists to use when you get to the store.

Be sure to give your children many opportunities to experiment with paper, crayons, pencils and safe markers. Show your children how to put their name on the paper by using a capital for the first letter and lower case letters for the rest.

How Does this Help My Child?

As children develop vocabulary and fine motor coordination, they move from early scribbling, to pictures, to strings of pretend letters, to real letters. Language development, including making pictures and prewriting skills, is an important part of school readiness.

39. How Much Time Before We Get There?

"How much longer before we get there? How many more days before my birthday?" Young children often have a difficult time waiting because time can't be touched, seen, heard, tasted, or smelled.

Materials:
paper
crayons
scissors

What to do:

Difficult concepts like time are much easier for children to understand when they are involved in drawing, cutting, pasting, counting, discussing, and moving something.

Decide on a picture or symbol to represent a length of time. If you will be riding in the car for several hours, children can draw and cut out cars representing each half hour. The cars can be taped somewhere in the car and removed as each time period passes. Then you and the children can count how much time is left.

The time before holidays or family visits can seem endless for children. A week before an event, cut out symbols for the holiday and line them up on a window. Every morning take down one object and place it in a basket. Then count how many objects are left on the window.

Adults can help children put something up to mark time instead of taking something down.

As an example, for Christmas you can create a paper tree for a window and place paper ornaments on the tree.

If people are coming for a visit, you can draw faces representing visitors. (This is a good practice for making circles and line segments.) Adults can print the visitors' names using correct upper and lower case letters under each one.

Adults can make a calendar and cross off days before a big event. This is a good time to start learning days of the week because children learn more quickly when information is important to them.

40. Fun with the ABC's

Teach your children to recognize upper and lower case letters during playtime.

Materials:
"ABC song"
ABC library books
Public Television shows
play dough
computer

What to do:

Sing the ABC song at every opportunity and read books about the ABC's to help begin the process of letter recognition. Young children will soon be singing with you. Once they know the song, take turns filling in the next letter when someone stops singing. Your library has many beautiful ABC books for you to share while singing.

Take out the play dough to make letters. Roll out "snakes" and make the letters of their names. Then move on to other letters, first capitals then lower case. Keep the playtime short and fun.

The computer is another way to teach letters. PBS.org and sesame street.org have many prereading games. Use a conventional font and set the size to 72. Supervise young children while they type, using the space bar and delete key to type again. Children love typing the names of family members, addresses, and phone numbers. They also like to write short messages. Keep in mind that many eye specialists recommend limited computer use for young children. You can use the keyboard without the screen for a "Search the Keyboard" game.

What else can I do?

Watch public education television shows together like "Sesame Street®" and "Super Why". Answer the characters' questions, and sing along.

Cooking with letters is fun. You can use peanut butter or frosting to make letters on cookies, crackers, pancakes, or bread.

Look for letters in newspaper headlines, signs, and play the game "I Spy with my Little Eye" when you're out in the community.

41. Nonfiction Books: a Vocabulary Goldmine

Children's nonfiction (true) books are filled with pictures, new vocabulary, and fascinating facts. They prepare young children to be curious enthusiastic students who search for information.

Materials:
a library card
a few interesting nonfiction library books

What to do:

When your child shows an interest in something, browse that library book section. Also, go to www.google.com/images, www.bing.com, or www.Youtube.com. Search for pictures, web sites, and short videos about the topic. (On-line sites can have inappropriate materials. Watch your spelling and check out sites in advance.) Children can practice finding and typing letters on the computer keyboard as you spell them.

Here are a few more tips:

Look for nonfiction books with many colorful pictures and captions. Since there are often too many details for young children, read the captions and summarize the text.

If it's an animal book, learn about habitats, life cycle, food, characteristics, and predators. For other subjects find the answers to who, what, when, where, why, and how?

Sketch pictures from the book and print a caption together.

What else can I do?

Stop and observe things while on neighborhood walks. If you see an ant, check it out. Ask a lot of questions and look up more information on insects. If you have a magnifying glass, REALLY check it out. Sketch what you see. Who cares if your child's sketch doesn't look exactly like an ant? You are modeling scientific curiosity and journal reporting found on TV programs like "Sid the Science Kid" on PBS.

A great children's gift is a small backpack with a magnifying glass, a drawing pad, ruler, tweezers, crayons, colored pencils, and a few small zip- lock bags for collecting.

42. Geometric Shapes

Young children love learning to recognize and use different geometric shapes to draw pictures. These skills help with reading, printing, math, and fine motor skills.

Materials:
napkins
play dough
crayons
paper

What to do:

Search for geometric shapes like a line segment (a piece of a line), rectangle, square, rhombus (diamond), circle, semi circle, triangle, trapezoid (a triangle with the top cut off), octagon (eight sided stop sign) and pentagon (five sided house) outside or in the house. Breakfast cereals and snacks are good examples of shapes. Pretzel sticks are good line segments. When passing out the snacks, hold up Cheerios and crackers and use the correct geometric term, "What do you want today, circles or squares?"

Octagon stop signs are fun to look for and talk about. While driving or walking around play "I Spy with my Little Eye" and use the correct names. Grandparents and parents can create shapes with their young ones while waiting for restaurant food. Fold a napkin or paper towel into a rectangle, triangle, and square. Point out the number of sides and corners (vertices). Trace the bottom of a cup and later use a children's scissors to practice cutting it in half for a semi circle.

Cut sandwiches into four triangles or one rhombus (diamond). Young children can cut bananas into circles and semi circles with a table knife. Point out that circles have no corners. "Do you think circles roll or slide?"

Play dough is also handy for making shapes. First, make line SEGMENTS. (A line continues into infinity in both directions.) Once children have made some worm shaped line segments, gently help them create the other shapes and combine shapes to make animals and food.

Check out Ed Emberley's series of drawing books, which add geometric shapes step by step to draw anything young children can imagine.

43. Playing Cars and Learning Geography

Here is a way to play cars with a geography and economics twist.

Materials:
a rug or tablecloth
small cars and trucks
boots and shoes
bowls
pots and pans
blue paper
scissors

What to do:

Find a U.S. map that shows different colors for landforms. Go to Google® or Bing® and search for "landform maps for kids."

On the floor or table, create a rug map of the United States.

Stuff snow boots, shoes, pots and pans under the rug to make geographic features.

Place big boots along the west side of the rug to create the younger volcanic type Rockies with high peaks and low valleys. Leave the rug flat along the Pacific Ocean coastline. Place shoes under the rug's east side for the older and lower Appalachian and Smoky Mountains. The middle is flat for the Plains. Near the top, place blue paper for the five Great Lakes. Make winding rivers down the mountains and hills draining into the lakes. (Water always travels down hill). Cut a long strip for the Mississippi River starting in northern Minnesota and ending in New Orleans. Construct bridges out of folded newspapers and Legos®.

Now start the playtime story. The cars travel around hills and over mountains on their way to Grandma's. Sometimes cars camp for the night. There are floods, damaged bridges, or road construction.

Trucks quickly carry Lego® food from farms to stores before it spoils. Trucks carry lumber, cars, and toys to stores. Garbage trucks carry wastes to landfill. Fire trucks, ambulances, and police come to the res-cue. Sometimes police even hand out speeding tickets.

How will this help my child?

This playtime encourages conversation, imagination, geographic and economic understanding of how goods and services move to their town. These activities can be done on the beach or in the snow too.

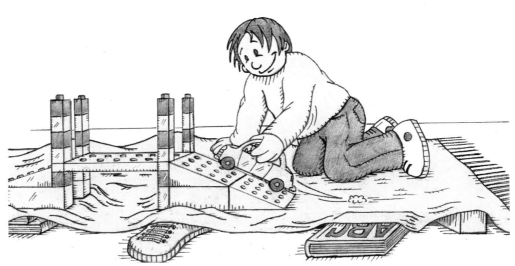

44. Playing Store and Learning Opportunity Cost

Playing store teaches personal finance lessons.

Materials:
cash register
money
merchandise
small box and string for a scanner
shopping bags
sale signs
price tags
clerk's name tag
a newspaper

What to do:
Price items and display them. Discuss how to sort materials according to categories and colors so they look organized and attractive. Have a conversation about what items will be popular and why. Does the display look nice?

Gather stuffed animals and dolls to go shopping with you. Make some paper $1 bills to spend or use play money.

Take turns choosing items and checking out. Have enough money for some items and not enough for others so the shopper is forced to make choices.

Adults can pretend to be disappointed that there isn't enough money for two desired items. Model how to work through the problem without a tantrum by thinking out loud, "Oh well, maybe I can buy this later. I'll save up my money."

This is **Opportunity cost,** choosing one thing between several equally desired ones. This important economic concept teaches children that sometimes you just can't have everything you want. You need to choose one item and give up another.

Think of other real situations to role-play. Look at newspaper ads. Have a sale. Have difficulty getting some merchandise. Call up the manufacturer or trucking company to teach how stores get items on the shelves.

When interest wanes, pack up the store for later.

How will this help my child?

Learning responsible personal finance begins early. Teaching **opportunity cost** and practicing the concept of **"maybe later"** help with other experiences in life when children must make difficult choices.

45. Cooking up Math and Reading Skills

Cooking with children provides many opportunities for math, reading directions carefully, thinking out loud, conversation, and quiet time activity.

Materials:

a recipe
apron or large towel

What to do:

Let children choose from several recipe options, preferably with pictures.

Place a chair next to the counter for young children to stand on so they have the proper height and a good view.

Slowly read through the recipe together. Emphasize the importance of reading the directions. Stop from time to time to discuss something and ask questions.

Wash hands thoroughly with soap as long as it takes to sing the ABC song. Gather materials together. Point out measuring instruments you will use like a cup, ½ cup, teaspoon, tablespoon, spatula, scraper, different size bowls, and pans.

Gather ingredients and explain the purpose and origin of each one. Example: use a map to show that most chocolate comes from Africa.

Read through the recipe carefully and follow directions. Young ones love to stir. Gently offer help when needed. Keep the experience successful and fun.

Set the timer and clean up together. Return all ingredients to their proper places, wash the dishes, counter top, and chair. Sample your product together and wrap some up for a friend.

Young children also love to make and serve salads. Children can use a table knife to cut celery, tomatoes, tiny carrots, tear lettuce, and toss in a few peas and nuts.

Making sandwiches together teaches sequence and how to safely use a table knife. Cut the bread into geometric shapes like rectangles, circles, squares, triangles, and pentagons.

Young children can also make snacks by spreading peanut butter, or cheese, and adding raisins on apples, celery, pears or whole-wheat crackers. They can mix different cereals, crackers, and dried fruit together for a quick trail mix.

46. Teaching Wise Money Management

The lifelong process of responsible personal finance (save, donate, spend, and invest) begins at a very early age.

Materials:

piggy bank or home made "banking system"

some real money

What to do:

For a homemade banking system, label three see- through plastic containers with SAVE, DONATE and SPEND WISELY.

An award winning transparent plastic piggy bank with sections labeled SAVE, DONATE, SPEND, AND INVEST is available on line. Search for Money Savvy Piggy Banks.

Grandparents can help fill the bank with coins when they visit. Remember to supervise children handling money.

Empty the bank together, add to the stash, and count it. Sort pennies, nickels, dimes, and quarters into piles using proper names.

Because pennies are worth "one", they can be used to practice counting.

Count the coins together as you place them back in the bank. Learning to say a number each time a coin is moved or dropped in the bank is an important skill. Very young children can practice counting to ten and start over again. Supervise dropping equal amounts of money in each section or they'll learn to put most of their money in the spend section.

Adults can have a short conversation about money. What have young children given to help others at church, charities, or the Humane Society? Are they saving for something special? How will they spend their money?

What else can I do?

Adults and children can make a piggy bank statement together.

Adults can add up the money in front of young children and tell them the total.

47. Learning Charity: Donating Time and Treasure

Donating time and treasure is an important part of teaching personal finance. Encouraging responsibility, volunteerism, self worth, and caring helps to make the world a better place. Well-rounded and healthy children give time and treasure to others.

What to do:

Discuss values important to your family. List what you like to do in your community. Discuss ways your family can help sustain those activities.

Religious and Special Needs Donations and Activities

Children can donate weekly and help with special disaster fundraisers. It helps them feel useful.

Compassion Toward Animals

The Humane Society has programs to buy food and toys for sheltered animals.

The School Family

Schools often have fundraisers to help families, and plan activities to make the school a better place. Children can help pick out warm clothing or extra school supplies for those in need. Teach young children to look for others who need a little extra help and kindness in the classroom.

Veterans and Grandparents

Young children can make art projects, write

letters and thank you notes to let adults know they are appreciated and loved during visits any time of the year.

Places You Visit

Museums, libraries, and other places you visit have fund drives where families can buy bricks or plaques to keep the facility open. Teach children to tidy up after they play at an exhibit.

Community Help

Communities need donations to build playgrounds, have fireworks, and provide other activities your family enjoys.

Sport teams, newspapers, and military groups have fundraisers and donation times for clothing, food, and toys.

Together you can bring articles to St. Vincent DePaul, the Salvation Army, or other thrift stores throughout the year.

Before giving money to charities on-line or TV, check out the percentage given to actual good works at charitywatch.org.

Helping Out

Bring a garbage bag on outings. If there is a mess, clean it up.

48. Raising Money Savvy Children: Planned Spending

Teaching young children good personal finance such as planned spending avoids ugly store scenes and creates good life-long spending habits.

Materials:
grocery list
"green" bag

What to do:

Adults can take one child at a time on a grocery store outing and teach how to trade money for food. (Going to a toy store is asking for trouble until wise planned spending is taught.)

Go through cupboards, gather coupons, and write a simple shopping list with your child (printed clearly). Point out that you shop from a list because stores have many ways to encourage more spending. Discuss what items are needed and how you will trade money for food.

Then explain that food comes from farms. It doesn't just appear on shelves. The farmer grows food and brings it to stores. It is sometimes packaged first. Then it goes to a trucker who brings food to the store. People work very hard to put food on the shelves and keep stores clean.

Visiting a Farmers' Market is also a good experience. While there you can talk to people who actually grow food.

While shopping, read labels and explain how to pick out the best quality fruit and vegetables without handling or sampling. Your child can pick out favorite foods on the list, take the merchandise to the counter, and give the money to the clerk. Explain the whole check out procedure. Pack the food in the "green" bag you have brought, take the slip, and change. A "thank you" and a smile teaches courtesy to clerks, too. Then and only then is the merchandise yours.

Back at home wash some food and while eating, review what you just did and why.

Children's Museums often have a store to help role-play grocery shopping.

49. Some Toys Teach Many Skills

Start looking at toys differently. Some toys have only one play dimension and are quickly forgotten. Others encourage imagination and teach many skills as young children develop.

Suggested Toys:
colored blocks that fit together

What can I do?

Large Lego®-type blocks can be used to teach sorting by color and size. The blocks help practice counting. Count piles while moving each block. At first, limit the number of blocks at playtime so that your child is successful. Add more blocks to count. Use piles of blocks to create rectangles and square buildings of different sizes. The blocks can also be used to make animals and designs for tracing with crayons on paper.

Playing with pieces like Legos® is important for developing small muscles in the fingers later used for writing. When children build, they use small muscles to twist and fit blocks together. Build different bases to produce the tallest and sturdiest tower. Compare height or length of different block stacks. Which is the tallest of the towers? Put them in order from shortest to tallest.

Adults can make stacks with a certain color sequence and children can copy the same sequence with blocks.

Lego® buildings can create the setting for a favorite book or made up story like the "Three Little Pigs", good and bad Nascars, or favorite princesses. Adults can start the story and then ask, "What happens next?"

For fun, children can build in a dishpan or little outdoor pool filled with water. Count how many interlocking blocks are needed to sink a little plastic storage container. You can also create an underwater story.

Adults and children can clean up by putting blocks in a container according to color or size and counting as they are dropped in.

50. Reading Picture Books

Books with few words but beautiful pictures are fantastic for story telling and developing conversation skills. Often children who are read to, develop good reading habits. No TV show, video, or computer game can replace two people reading together and talking.

Materials:
Your librarian can recommend picture books with few words.

What to do:
Find a cozy spot for reading

After reading the title, author, and illustrator, start a conversation. Soak in the beauty of the pages by looking at the pictures. Start making up a story using your own words and the book's illustrations. Your child will learn to add to the story.

Ask questions that begin with what, who, where, when, why do you think, or how? How do the characters feel—happy, sad, angry, upset, lonely, warm or cuddly inside? What is the character thinking? What will the character do next? Name the characters.

After you have exhausted those questions, ask "What do you think will happen next?" Predicting is an important reading skill.

Whatever you do, take it slow and relax. Adults often hurry children. Give them time to think. Relax. Reading calms children and adults, preparing for sleep, soothing a hurt, and giving great joy. This is an extremely important part of every child's routine before naps and bedtime.

Here are a few award winning picture book authors and titles: *Tuesday, The Three Pigs, Flotsam, Free Fall,* and *Sector 7 by Wiesner;* Lehman's *The Red Book, Museum Trip, Rainstorm,* and *Trainstop;* Rathmann's *Good Night, Gorilla,* and *10 Minutes till Bedtime;* Briggs' *The Snowman;* VanAllsburg's *Ben's Dream;* Blake's *Clown;* dePaola's *Pancakes for Breakfast;* Spiers' *Rain;* Rohmann's *Time Flies; Deep in the Forest* by Turkle; *The Silver Pony* by Ward; *Yellow Umbrella* by Jae-Soo Liu; and *Hug* by Alborough.

51. City Bus Trips Help Children Learn

Sometimes young children and their caregivers REALLY need to get out of the house on a gloomy day. Taking a city bus trip with some suggested activities is an inexpensive outing that teaches many skills. It helps young children chase away the "left behind" feeling at the beginning of the school year. No special destination is required.

Materials:
bus schedule
city map from the telephone book
tickets or necessary change
snacks that won't be messy

What to do:

In advance, call the bus station for the schedule, closest bus stop, cost, and rules for snacks. Many cities have all the information online. If your community does not have a bus, you could use public transportation when you visit a larger community. It is a cheap way to go exploring without the hassle of driving. Buses will often go past museums and other community stops, but you can stay aboard and ride the bus just for the fun of it.

Keep the trip short (less than an hour) unless you plan a toilet break.

Because objects may be zooming by, keep the activities simple. Depending upon the children's ages, look for objects of a certain color, count the number of white trucks, stop signs, and traffic lights. You could even count gas stations. Together look for different shapes like a square, rectangle, rhombus (diamond), trapezoid, circle, octagon (stop sign) and triangle. You could also play an alphabet game spotting the letters of the alphabet in order.

Help teach simple economics by pointing out delivery trucks bringing goods to stores and people unloading boxes. Explain that merchandise doesn't just appear on shelves; it takes trucks, many people, and hard work to get food and merchandise in stores.

Look for police cars, city workers, mail carriers, emergency vehicles, school buses, and package delivery trucks. Explain what they are doing and that it takes many people working together to make a community. Your librarian can find many books about these community occupations.

Adults can teach a little geography, too. Point out hills, rivers, highways, turns in the road, intersections, bridges, and other features. Use a route map to show children where you are and track your progress.

52. Inside Fun and Dramatic Play

Children of all ages love to make a special cozy place to play. Outside, kids build forts or set up tents. On a day when it is better to be inside, you can help them set up a little box train, tent or hideaway place.

Materials:

cardboard boxes of various sizes
paper plate
markers
sofa cushions
pillows
two chairs or a card table
snacks
flashlight

What to do:

For a quiet activity, spread a big sheet over chairs or card table. Inside the tent, let your children make a little room with their favorite blanket, pillow, books and toys. Sometimes, little kids can fit into a tunnel simply made with sofa cushions placed against a solid surface. Send in a non-sticky snack like crackers or cheerios. A flashlight adds extra fun.

For a more active time, use cardboard boxes to make a play train. The boxes can vary in size as long as your child can sit in them. Each box is a different car. Markers can be used to draw wheels and lights for the engine. A paper plate can be made into a steering wheel. Kids love to take turns being the engineer and passengers.

Support the activity by pretending and carrying on a conversation, especially if there is only one child.

How Will This Help My Child?

Imaginative play builds vocabulary, problem solving and communication skills. Children playing in a "tent" are learning to control their environment, problem solve, as well as develop an appreciation for quiet activities. Reading and dramatic play should always be done with the TV OFF. It is very hard for a child to use imagination when the television is distracting.

53. Indoor Bubbles

Science activities, such as playing with bubbles, help young children learn to ask questions and make predictions. Here's a way to play with bubbles indoors with very little mess.

Materials:

dish detergent
water
plastic straw
camera
measuring tape
paper and pencil
counter top

What to do:

Clean a counter top. Wet the counter top with about 1/8 cup of water and spread it around the counter. Place a drop of dish detergent on the counter and spread around with your hand until you have bubbles.

Wet the straw tip in your bubble solution. Gently place the tip where the bubble meets the counter and slowly blow. The bubble will enlarge as long as it stays in the soapy solution. Measure the diameter of the bubbles. To make smaller bubbles inside larger bubbles, dip the straw in the solution and gently blow inside the larger bubble.

Children can try different techniques for producing bubbles. Discuss what works and what doesn't work. What happens if you change the angle of the straw? What colors do you see in the bubbles? What color does the bubble become the moment before it bursts? Who can make the most bubbles inside a larger bubble? Can you move the bubble? Predict what will happen if you move the bubble to a dry spot? Can you pick it up?

Adults may need a little background on bubbles to help answer questions. When children blow air into bubbles, the soap solution stretches. We see colors when light bends. The thinnest part of the bubble turns red. When the bubble pops the air rushes out.

What else can I do?

Take pictures of your science activity and write a bubble story together.

54. Math Fun and Finger Foods

Counting is much more than memorizing a sequence of numbers. Matching one number to one object is real counting and will take practice. Children often double count and skip numbers for a long time.

Materials:
cereal
crackers
chocolate chip cookies
raisin bread
linked blocks
other objects around the house

What to do

Adults can teach number meaning very casually at meal and snack times. Count out a few food items as you place them on a plate. Gently help children count while MOVING food like cereal, pieces of bread, fruit, vegetables, or cheese. Keep the activity fun. Children can also count as they distribute, eat each piece of food, or help clear the table.

Counting can also be used to check how many pieces of food remain. "How many more pieces of corn do you have left on the plate? " Be sure to use a number they can count successfully. When children master the lower numbers, continue with the next few numbers. (Mastering means your child does a skill very easily and naturally.)

Count during daily activities. Sort light and dark clothes and count items placed in the washer. Count while straightening the house. Count while playing or traveling in the car. Games such as "Chutes and Ladders®" reinforce math skills as children count and move play pieces around the board.

What else can I do?

Children love to use a fork to mine for chocolate chips in cookies or raisins in raisin bread and count them. It's messy eating but adds variety to counting play.

55. Storytelling

Young children love to hear stories about parents and grandparents' childhood. It is their first exposure to history, ancestors, and stories of people they love. Most important, if family stories are passed on, they are not lost.

What to do:

Each generation passes on family values, morals, and religion through stories and conversation. They are lessons of kindness, sharing, perseverance, courage, and triumph over difficulty. Some are just funny.

Telling stories takes a little practice. Start with a story you know well. Perhaps your grandparents told you some stories. Think back to an encounter with an animal, an experience you remember vividly, something funny, a lesson you learned, or a slightly scary story that turns out well. Use lots of descriptions and sound effects. Be sure to use gestures and don't be afraid to exaggerate.

There might be a favorite book, Aesop's fable, legend, or Bible story that teaches a lesson you want your children to remember. Take out old family pictures and tell their story. These stories are great for car trips, long winter nights, family holidays, or times when children need to settle down.

Parents and children can tape record interviews with grandparents to ensure stories and voices live on. Have the questions written in advance and practice with the technology. Grandparents can receive questions in advance to think about their answers. Young children can press the buttons and help ask questions. "What is your name and do you know why you have it? When were you born? What did the family do for fun? What family chores did you do? How has technology changed? What were your favorite foods? What is your favorite funny family story? What were your special holiday traditions? Were there any fads while growing up? Were there any special home remedies when the family got sick?" The interviews can be made into CD's and given as gifts.

56. Nutritious Facts and Food

According to a study by scientists at University College London (International Journal of Obesity 2010), children who are cared for by grandparents full time are up to 34% more likely to be overweight than their peers. Young children with grandparents may be overfed with fatty and sugary treats and less likely to take part in physical games.

Suggestions

According to a 2009 national study, there are four behaviors that help young children remain healthy:

Eat nutritious meals six or seven times per week with the family at a table, watch less than two hours of TV per day, sleep 10.5 hours per night, and exercise a total of one hour per day.

To help develop daily diets, snacks, and learn about the government food pyramid for young children go to MyPyramid.gov.

Here are some suggestions to help raise healthy children:

• Read labels. Read labels. Read labels. The first few ingredients are the most abundant in packaged food. Choose food with least amount of salt and sugar (all kinds sugar) and the highest amount of fiber and nutrients on the label.

• American Heart Association suggests teaching children to reach for water first to quench thirst. Fruit juices, such as orange and apple, are a source of calories that add up quickly.

• Serve more vegetables and fruits and make them appealing to children.

• Encourage physical play and avoid offering food as a reward.

• Decrease the amount of sugar or honey in a recipe by ½. Just add a little more vanilla.

• Choose frozen rather than canned fruits and vegetables.

• Don't offer dessert as the final part of every meal. Offer dessert just a few times a week.

• If you give treats, offer fruit, vegetables, string cheese, low sugar cereal, or crackers and WATER.

- Pack bags of healthy snacks for trips.
- Explain why you say "no" to unhealthy food.
- Check peanut butter labels. Choose the one that simply has peanuts. That's it!
- Don't keep "junk food" or soda in the house.
- Clean out your cupboards and refrigerator. Stock healthy foods: fruits, vegetables, yogurt (with doctor ok) low sugar and low salt crackers, eggs, low salt cheese, cottage cheese, chicken and other meat, peanut butter and nuts (when your doctor gives the ok), milk, whole wheat bread foods and pasta.
- **Check with your doctor for suggestions and the MyPyramid.gov site.**

Make Fruits and Vegetables Tasty for Young Children

Here are some suggestions:
- Low fat cream cheese on celery, thin sliced summer squash, zucchini, or cucumbers and top with raisins (Peanut butter can be used with your doctor's ok)
- Low fat cream cheese and crushed or finely chopped fruit on a cracker or toast
- Bananas, apples, and other fruit in pancakes
- Apples cut in thin circles with a little cinnamon
- Fresh or frozen berries
- Red sweet pepper strips
- Frozen or fresh banana (They can be dipped in a LITTLE chocolate and granola.)
- Cut up oranges, grapefruit, grapes, pineapple, melons in different shapes–circles, wedges, triangles
- Applesauce (Check labels for no sugar.)
- Dip fruit and vegetables in plain or vanilla yogurt (when approved by doctor)
- Cherry tomatoes
- Frozen berries or grapes on a hot day (if your child is old enough)
- Carrots cut like potato chips
- Fruit kabobs dipped in yogurt
- Fruit smoothies (fruit, vanilla yogurt and a little milk in a blender)
- Fruit cubes or pops (Prepare as a smoothie and freeze in an ice cube with a strong tooth pick holder, cupcake, or popsicle tray with a stick as a holder)

Check out the excellent book *Taming of the C.A.N.D.Y Monster* by Vicki Lansky (1999) for more suggestions and recipes.

57. Great Gifts and Home Supplies for Fun and Learning

When birthdays and holidays come around, parents and grandparents often want to give a special gift. While there are many expensive electronic and mechanical toys available, often their favorite toys are simple and easy to use. Appropriate toys for young children should encourage discovery, learning, and creativity. They should be sturdy and easily handled by little fingers.

Recommended toys and supplies:

• All kinds of art/craft supplies like pencils, drawing paper, crayons, washable markers and paints (with supervision), child scissors, glue, colored paper.
• Play dough (store bought or made at home) and little rolling pins, cutters, etc.
• Easy wooden puzzles.

• Large plastic connecting pieces like giant Legos®, Duplo® (Regular sized Lego® blocks have too many little pieces for very young children.)
• Bath toys.
• Magnetic alphabet letters and number (with supervision).
• Easy to catch balls for inside and outside. Inflatable beach balls work well inside during cold months.
• Large cardboard building blocks—perfect for stacking and making all sorts of roads, towers, etc. (Search for Giant Building Block sets by Imagiday, Imagibricks or Melissa Basic Cardboard Blocks.)
• Sandbox and snow toys—plastic pails, shovels, diggers, trucks, etc.
• Simple to move cars and trucks.
• Baby dolls.
• Simple musical instruments like whistles, drums, and horns.

- CDs with children's stories and songs.
- Play tools.
- Items for playing dress-up.
- Magnifying glass.
- Piggy banks (Savvy Pig).
- Inside play tent.
- Snuggly blanket and stuffed animals.
- Board games like Candy Land® and Chutes and Ladders® and card games like Go Fish®

We also recommend BOOKS! BOOKS! BOOKS! Children need to be read to several times each day.

Look for books that introduce the alphabet, colors, shapes other beginning concepts in a creative way such as *Now I Eat My ABC's* by Abrams, *Pets ABC* by Dahl, *Achoo! Bang! Crash!* By MacDonald, *Chicka Chicka Boom Boom* by Martin, *Click, Clack* by Cronin and *Mouse Paint* by Walsh, *10 Little Rubber Ducks* by Carle, *Counting Kisses* by Katz, *Shapes* by Crowther,

Too Big, Too Small, Just Right by Minters, *I Stink!* by McMullan, *Yes* and other books by Alborough, and *What Will Fat Cat Sit On?* by Thomas, *Llama, Llama* by Dewdney, *Can You Growl Like a Bear?* by Butler, *Sheep in a Jeep* by Shaw and Apple, *Chickens to the Rescue* by Hillelman, *Corduroy* by Freeman, *Moon* books by Asch, *Very Hungry Caterpillar* and other stories by Eric Carle, word books by Richard Scarry, *Where's Spot?* by Hill, *Go Dog Go!, Put Me in the Zoo* and other titles by Seuss or Eastman.

Check book lists at your library, the All-Time Best Books for Preschoolers, or Top Books for Toddlers at www.parents.com.

The Authors

Learning Through the Seasons is a project of Grandparents Teach, Too, a nonprofit organization founded by early elementary teachers, reading specialists, and early childhood specialists, Iris Katers, Esther Macalady, Cheryl Anderegg, Jean Hetrick, and Tim Fox. They can be reached at grandparentsteach @gmail.com or their web site www.grandparentsteachtoo.org.

To order additional copies:

Grandparents Teach, Too
15 Specker Circle, Marquette, Michigan 49855
906-228-9183
For book cost and shipping information:
grandparentsteach@gmail.com or www.grandparentsteachtoo.org